ENDANGERED AND EXTINCT
ANIMALS OF THE
FORESTS

Michael Bright

FRANKLIN WATTS
London · Sydney

© Aladdin Books Ltd 2001

Produced by:
Aladdin Books Ltd
28 Percy Street
London W1P 0LD

ISBN 0–7496–4411–7

First published in Great Britain in 2001 by:
Franklin Watts
96 Leonard Street
London EC2A 4XD

Editor:
Kathy Gemmell

272718

Designer:
Flick, Book Design & Graphics

Illustrators:
Cy Baker, Tim Bramfitt,
James Field (SGA), Peter
Hayman, Mike Lacey (SGA),
Mick Loates, Sean Milne, Terry
Riley (SGA), Raymond Turvey,
Mike Unwin, Ross Watton (SGA),
Maurice Wilson
Cartoons: Jo Moore

Certain illustrations have
appeared in earlier books
created by Aladdin Books.

Printed in Belgium
A CIP catalogue record for this
book is available from the
British Library.

Contents

Introduction

The world's forests are disappearing at an alarming rate. An area of tropical rainforest the size of Wales is destroyed every year.

The trees are felled for timber or cleared for agriculture. As the forests go, so do the animals that live in them. With their living space reduced and their food gone, many are now endangered. Some are already extinct – they have disappeared forever. Forests can be replanted, but the goodness in the soil has already been used up, and the new trees do not grow well. Today's surviving forests now contain some of the rarest animals in the world.

Q: Why watch out for these boxes?

A: They answer important questions about extinct and endangered wildlife.

zoom in on...

Bits and pieces

Look out for these boxes to take a closer look at features of certain animals.

Awesome facts

Watch out for these dodo diamonds to learn more weird and wonderful facts about endangered and extinct animals and their world.

Endangered and extinct

When few animals of a particular species survive in the wild, it is said to be endangered. If a species disappears altogether, it is extinct. Some extinctions are caused by human activities. Others are caused by natural events, like changes in climate or sea level, volcanic eruptions or competition from similar animals.

SYMBOL DEFINITIONS

In this book, the red cross symbol shows an animal that is already extinct. The yellow exclamation shows an animal that is endangered. Animals that are less endangered are said to be 'vulnerable'. Those that are more endangered and close to extinction are considered to be 'critically endangered'. The green tick shows an animal that has either been saved from the brink of extinction or has recently been discovered. Many of these 'success' stories, however, are still endangered species.

American ivory-billed woodpecker

Fruit bat

Arabian oryx

Animals that have been introduced into a particular habitat, accidentally or on purpose, are called alien animals. Cats, for example, are taken overseas by humans to places where they do not occur naturally. If they breed, they attack and kill the resident animals and can cause them to become extinct.

Q: Does it matter if some animals become extinct?

A: Yes. Every plant and animal on Earth is important. Each has its role to play in the natural order. Removing one upsets the order and affects other living things. The overall picture of life on Earth – the variety of plants and animals, their behaviour and the ways in which they interact – is called biodiversity. Maintaining biodiversity is essential for the survival of all species.

The Guadeloupe amazon was an early victim of human exploitation. It was safely isolated on its West Indian island from mainland predators. Then sailors and plantation owners arrived. They cleared the forests and ate the birds. The species was extinct by 1750.

For many years, people hunted wild animals without reducing stocks substantially. They understood the ways of the forest and did not take too much too often. Then others started to catch or kill too many animals. Animals such as tigers became scarce. This increased their value, so that even when they were protected, hunters were prepared to catch them illegally. This is called poaching.

Our closest relatives: the apes

All living apes are forest dwellers and are threatened by logging, poaching and disturbance. Many of the African apes live in war zones, where they are killed by soldiers or desperate people hunting for food. Their Asian relatives often die in forest fires lit deliberately to clear land for agriculture.

There are two types of gorilla – lowland and mountain. They are found in Africa's rainforests, where they live in peaceful family groups, feeding on fruits and foliage. They are killed illegally for their meat and for a detestable tourist trade in gorilla mementoes, such as gorilla-hand ashtrays.

Awesome facts
American researcher Dian Fossey tried to save Rwanda's mountain gorillas, but was killed by poachers. She is buried in the mountains next to her beloved gorillas.

The common chimpanzee was once found in the forests of 25 countries in West Africa. Now it lives in just five. It is caught alive and exported for the pet trade or killed for food. In the wild, there are now only between 100,000 and 200,000 chimpanzees left.

The orang-utan is a solitary fruit-eater that lives only on the islands of Borneo and Sumatra in Southeast Asia. Its forests are being destroyed by commercial logging and for agriculture. There is also a trade in the animals, both living and dead, with skulls fetching up to £100 each.

Q: What happens to baby apes when their mothers are killed?

A: Orphaned infants are often taken as pets and kept in appalling conditions. Many are sold to medical laboratories and zoos. Some are rescued and taken to orphanages, where they are taught how to live in the wild and then released.

African forest monkeys

Many species of African monkey are killed to be eaten. Scientists have recently learned that some diseases common in monkeys can also infect humans. This means that eating monkeys is not only bad for the monkeys, but can also be dangerous for us.

Sclater's guenon

!

zoom in on...

Bushmeat

Bushmeat is the name for wild animals killed for food. There is a thriving trade in bushmeat around logging camps in West Africa, to provide loggers with fresh food from the forest. This has caused a big increase in the number of monkeys and apes killed for their meat.

Sclater's guenon, a monkey from the Nigerian swamp forests, was thought to be extinct until 1988, when five small populations were found. Two are close to villages that consider them to be sacred and do not kill them. The other three are hunted heavily

8

Preuss's monkey

White-throated monkey

The forests of southwestern Nigeria and southern Benin are home to the white-throated monkey. It is hunted for meat, and its forests are being cleared. This species does not adapt well to the thinner forests and is fast dying out.

Preuss's monkey lives in the forests of western Cameroon, eastern Nigeria and the island of Bioko in Equatorial Guinea. It is losing its forest home to logging, so has started raiding crops, and is often killed by farmers.

Q: Are sacred monkeys safe?

A: In certain religions, such as Hinduism, it is forbidden to kill monkeys. In places where a monkey is sacred, it is relatively safe. However, some populations of sacred monkeys have been so successful that they have invaded homes and offices and become a nuisance. These ones are likely to be killed, sacred or not!

The Javan leaf monkey is one of several species of leaf monkey that live only on the island of Java in Indonesia. All are considered endangered due to loss of their habitat. Just four per cent of the island's original forest is still standing.

Asian forest monkeys

Monkeys in tropical Asia are seeing their forest homes disappear rapidly. In some places, such as Vietnam, Cambodia and Laos, up to 70 per cent of trees have been destroyed by wars, logging and clearance for agriculture. Some species have only recently been discovered, but are already on the way to extinction.

zoom in on

Wars and animals

Forests in Southeast Asia have been racked by war for many years. Chemicals that strip the leaves off trees, powerful explosives, firebombs and the fighters themselves have destroyed huge tracts of forest and wiped out the animals that live there.

In the remote limestone hills of northern Vietnam, conservation laws mean very little. Local people hunt monkeys, like the Tonkin snub-nosed monkey, for food and to use their body parts as ingredients in oriental medicines.

Coffee, tea and spice plantations have replaced the moist forests in India's Western Ghats (mountains), which are home to the endangered lion-tailed macaque. The monkeys are caught and sold illegally to research laboratories or zoos, or to be kept as pets.

Lion-tailed macaque

11

The endangered buffy tufted-eared marmosets of southeastern Brazil are found sleeping in tree branches in groups of a dozen or more. As their forest shrinks, these small primates are increasingly caught for the pet trade or biomedical research.

The black-faced lion tamarin is one of the world's rarest mammals. It was discovered on the island of Superagui in 1990, but illegal trade and the impact of agriculture has meant that, just over a decade later, it is now in danger of extinction.

Buffy tufted-eared marmoset

Awesome facts

The world's entire population of 500 golden-headed lion tamarins lives in Brazil's Una Biological Reserve, but much of the Reserve has now been destroyed by fire.

12

Brazilian forest monkeys

There were once huge rainforests along the Atlantic coast of Brazil, but today, much of the forest has been replaced by large cities, industries and cattle ranches. The monkeys living in them are all critically endangered and can only be saved from extinction by captive breeding.

zoom in on...

Teaching tamarins

Because some monkeys are confined to tiny patches of forest, any natural disaster, such as fire, has a huge impact on their survival. Some endangered monkeys, such as tamarins, are reared in captivity. When released, they are so unused to living in the wild that they have to be taught just about everything – including how to climb trees!

The aye-aye is a curious gremlin-like creature. It has a very thin, strangely elongated middle finger, which it uses to winkle out grubs from rotting wood. Its sensitive, bat-like ears can pick up the sound of grubs moving under tree bark. It is nocturnal (comes out at night) and is very rarely seen.

The golden bamboo lemur was discovered as recently as 1987, but is now the most endangered lemur on Madagascar. It lives near the village of Ranomafana in southeast Madagascar, but there are only 1,000 individuals left. The bamboo forests in which it lives and on which it feeds are being cleared for agriculture. It is also hunted for food, and youngsters are taken as pets.

Awesome factS
The golden bamboo lemur eats bamboo leaves containing poisons, such as cyanide, which would be lethal to any other animal.

Madagascar's vanishing lemurs

The island of Madagascar is the only place on Earth where primates called lemurs (meaning 'ghosts') are found. About 50 million years ago, Madagascar separated from mainland Africa, isolating the earliest lemurs. They adapted to the varied habitats in Madagascar to give us around 40 species today.

Arabia

India

Africa

Indian Ocean

Madagascar

zoom in on...

Isolation

When Madagascar separated from Africa, the lemurs were able to evolve (develop) in isolation from the mainland's monkeys and apes. Without this competition, they occupied all the habitats that monkeys would have taken. They thrived until people arrived, 2,000 years ago, with their cattle and goats, and modified the island's plant life. Lemurs began to have a hard time. Some species that live on the ground, such as the ring-tailed lemur (right) are common, but many species are endangered.

Tiger, tiger

Thousands of tigers were shot by hunters in the 19th century, and populations were reduced considerably. This was followed by widespread destruction of forests, which meant that the tigers' prey (food) disappeared and they starved. Tiger numbers all over Asia plummeted and are still falling. The tiger is now on the edge of extinction.

zoom in on...

Tiger medicine

A dead tiger is valuable to a hunter because it can be sold to the oriental medicine trade. Skin, bones, blood and body parts are thought to have mystical properties that cure all manner of diseases. Many tigers are killed illegally.

Eight subspecies of tiger once ranged from Turkey to the Pacific coast, but today, all are seriously threatened. With plantations and farms taking over tiger country, tigers and people have come into closer contact. Some have attacked people, and have been shot or poisoned. In India, Project Tiger was established in the 1960s to save the Bengal tiger, but in 2001 it has been acknowledged a failure.

and bathing to keep cool.

The smallest tiger, the Bali tiger, is extinct, and its close relatives, the Indochinese, Javan and Sumatran tigers, are critically endangered. The reddish-coloured South Chinese tiger may also be extinct.

Bali tiger

Awesome facts
In a single police 'sting' operation in New Delhi, India, 500kg of tiger bones destined for the oriental medicine trade were confiscated.

The Caspian tiger is on the critical list, and is unlikely to survive.

Forest giants

Some of the most recent discoveries of large mammals have been in tropical forests. Unfortunately, no sooner have they been found than they are considered to be under threat of extinction, because the forests in which they live are disappearing so quickly.

The 50,000 remaining Asian elephants are big animals and need a lot of space. However, with their forests being cleared, they have taken to crop raiding and are being killed for their trouble. Males are also slaughtered for their ivory tusks. Conservation measures include planting trees to provide corridors for the elephants between the fragmented forests.

The critically endangered Sumatran rhinoceros has been reduced by poaching to just 300 individuals. Its relative, the Javan rhino, is confined to two parks, one in Java and the other in Vietnam. The horns are valued as ingredients in oriental medicine. Surviving animals have been weakened by inbreeding. This means that certain flaws, such as low resistance to disease, are being passed from one generation to the next.

Giant rats

Most giant musk rats were wiped out from West Indian island forests by European settlers in the 1600s. But the Martinique musk rat, as big as a cat, survived until 1902, when the island's volcano erupted and wiped it out in clouds of poisonous gas.

zoom in on...

Q: Are there large mammals still to be discovered?

A: Yes. The forests of Vietnam, Laos and Cambodia, for example, have been hiding many large mammals. The giant muntjac was discovered in 1994, and the Vu Quang ox (left) in 1992. All are under pressure from hunting and forest destruction.

On the edge

The Cebu flowerpecker (below) was thought to be extinct until an expedition came across it in Tabunan Forest on the Philippines island of Cebu in 1992. The scientists discovered several other birds and bats that had been considered extinct. Their discovery makes these creatures some of the rarest animals in the world. They are vulnerable to any changes in their habitat.

Christmas Island in the Indian Ocean is known for its red land crabs, which are now falling prey to imported 'crazy' ants. But there were once several small mammals, too, such as Captain Maclear's rat (left), the Christmas Island musk shrew (below left) and the bulldog rat (below right). Black rats and cats that were introduced by miners came to dominate the islands and the local rats and shrews became extinct.

Fading island forests

When trees come down, it is not only large animals that suffer. Smaller creatures are disappearing too. Many snails, insects, small birds, mice and rats that live on the forest floor or in the leafy understorey are now vulnerable.

Hidden in the forests of Oahu in Hawaii, is the Oahu tree snail. This glossy mollusc was once found from sea level to mountain top, but when the forests below 300m were cleared, the snail disappeared with them. It survives on the higher slopes but is now considered to be endangered.

Awesome facts
There are six po'ouli birds left in the world on the Hawaiian island of Maui. There is now war against the rats that steal their eggs and chicks.

Hidden forest animals

Camouflaged in the undergrowth or the foliage of forest trees, many animals can escape being seen by their natural predators. However, when the forests are destroyed, they are vulnerable, as there is nowhere to hide.

The Malayan tapir lives close to rivers. During the construction of hydroelectric dams, which provide electricity to the area, many rivers were flooded. This submerged the places where the tapirs live.

The beautiful clouded leopard is hunted for its coat. It is a secretive and solitary cat that lives in the receding tropical forests of southern Asia. Its teeth and bones are ground up and used in oriental medicines.

zoom in on...

Slash and burn

Farmers in tropical areas cut down trees and burn undergrowth to clear plots of forest land for farming. But the forest's nutrients are stored mainly in the trees, and the crops soon drain any goodness from the treeless soil. Farmers then clear more forest to try again, until all the forest is gone.

to climb in and out of the water.

The maned sloth is endangered. It lives in the Atlantic coast forest of Brazil, where 97 per cent of the trees have been removed for timber and charcoal production. The sloth is hunted for the pet trade and killed for the medicinal properties it is thought to have.

The endangered Philippines spotted deer is no bigger than a dog. It lives in the forests of the Visayan Islands, but has been lost from most of its former range. Today, it survives on just two islands.

New Guinea is home to the endangered long-beaked echidna. It is a monotreme (a mammal that lays eggs) and is highly prized for food by the locals. It is hunted by specially trained dogs.

Dying down under

Several waves of human immigrants have had a great impact on Australia's wildlife. The first tribes to arrive brought dogs and, more recently, Europeans brought cattle, sheep and rabbits. With each invasion, habitats were altered and the new species ate or competed with the indigenous (local) wildlife, which is now dying out.

Q: How do forest fires affect wildlife?

A: Fire is essential for certain plants to reproduce. Burning enables them to release seeds. Animals generally escape the flames. In Australia, however, patterns of bush and forest fires have shifted due to global changes in the weather. Some of these fires kill rare wildlife.

The numbat is a termite-eating marsupial (pouched mammal) that is restricted to southwest Australia It was heavily preyed on by foxes introduced by European settlers

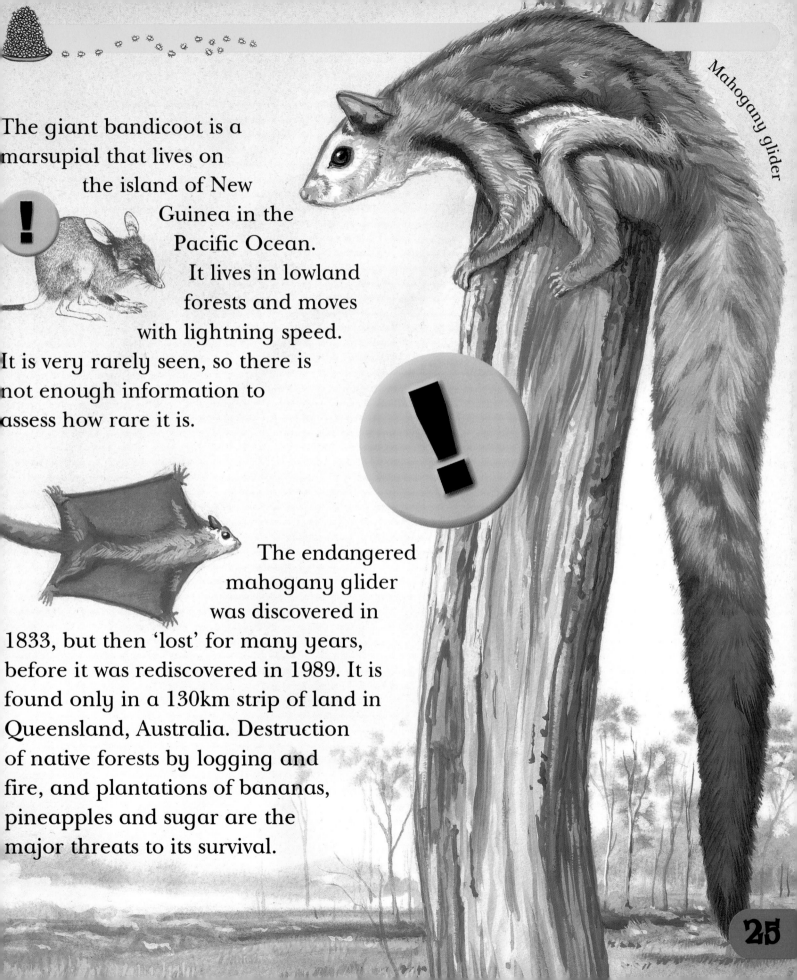

The giant bandicoot is a marsupial that lives on the island of New Guinea in the Pacific Ocean. It lives in lowland forests and moves with lightning speed. It is very rarely seen, so there is not enough information to assess how rare it is.

The endangered mahogany glider was discovered in 1833, but then 'lost' for many years, before it was rediscovered in 1989. It is found only in a 130km strip of land in Queensland, Australia. Destruction of native forests by logging and fire, and plantations of bananas, pineapples and sugar are the major threats to its survival.

Mahogany glider

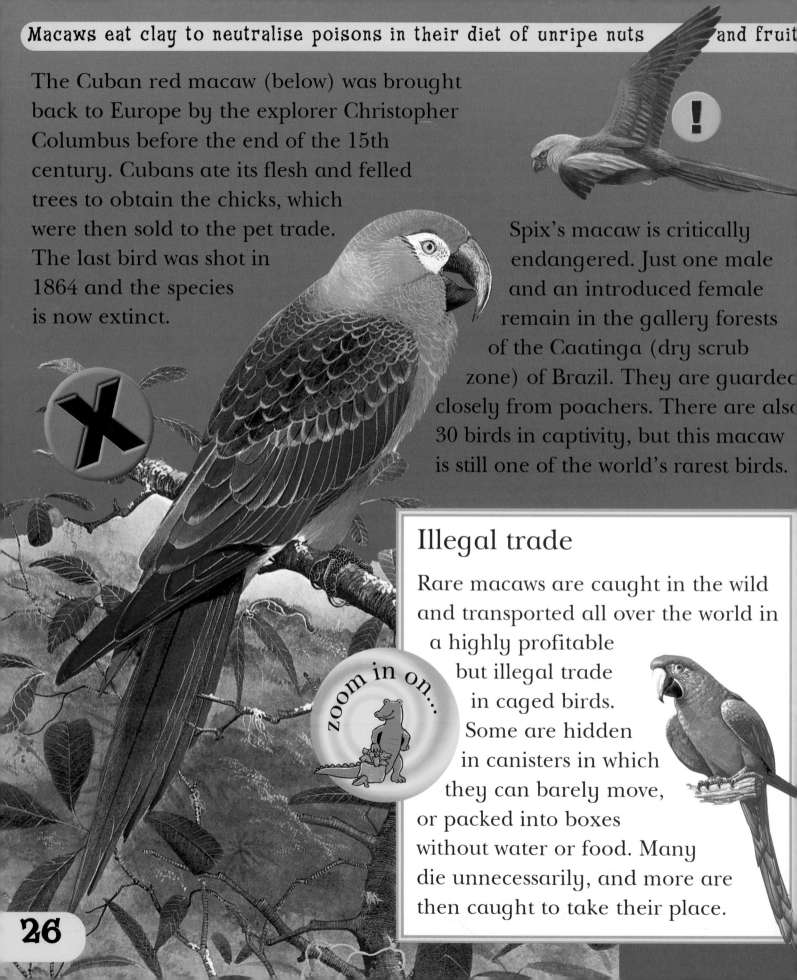

The Cuban red macaw (below) was brought back to Europe by the explorer Christopher Columbus before the end of the 15th century. Cubans ate its flesh and felled trees to obtain the chicks, which were then sold to the pet trade. The last bird was shot in 1864 and the species is now extinct.

Spix's macaw is critically endangered. Just one male and an introduced female remain in the gallery forests of the Caatinga (dry scrub zone) of Brazil. They are guarded closely from poachers. There are also 30 birds in captivity, but this macaw is still one of the world's rarest birds.

zoom in on...

Illegal trade

Rare macaws are caught in the wild and transported all over the world in a highly profitable but illegal trade in caged birds. Some are hidden in canisters in which they can barely move, or packed into boxes without water or food. Many die unnecessarily, and more are then caught to take their place.

The Norfolk Island kaka once fed on the nectar of the white hibiscus tree, and had a strange scoop-like adaptation of its tongue to lick out the sugary fluid. The last bird died in a cage in London in 1851.

The critically endangered Philippines cockatoo once lived throughout the Philippines, but today, just 1,000 birds survive on a few islands. The others were trapped for the pet trade or died out as forests were destroyed. Now the birds are also dying of fungal disease.

Passing parrots

Parrots have long been caught in the wild for the pet trade. People love their colourful plumage and ability to mimic human words. Some species have been in such demand that their numbers in the wild have crashed. The rarer a parrot becomes, the more valuable it is, making the problem worse.

Lost birds of the Americas

Unbelievably huge flocks of birds once flew across North America. It was said that there were so many in a flock that the sun was blotted out as the flock passed by. The huge flocks are now gone, with several species wiped out by hunters' guns.

The queleli was a carrion-eating falcon from the island of Guadalupe, off the coast of Baja California. It became extinct as a direct result of human activity. Introduced goats ate the island's plant life and herders poisoned the birds, claiming that they took baby goats. Introduced cats ate queleli chicks, and collectors wiped out the last few birds.

The Carolina parakeet was North America's only parrot. But the birds were hunted, kept as pets or killed by farmers because they ate farm seeds. The birds were easy to kill. If one was shot, the others gathered round to defend it, and they could then be shot, too.

Awesome factS

One flock of passenger pigeons contained more than a billion birds. It took more than three hours to pass overhead.

X

In the 19th century, the passenger pigeon was the world's most numerous bird. One breeding site was 64km long, and each tree held 100 nests. Hunting parties could shoot as many as 50,000 birds in a weekend. The population dropped quickly and the birds were extinct in the wild by 1900. The last captive bird, called Martha, died in Cincinnati Zoo in 1914.

Back from the dead

Some rare animals can be bred in captivity in zoos and parks and then released back into the wild. In a few cases, breeding techniques include implanting the eggs of rare species into more common species. The stand-in mothers bring up their rare offspring as if they were their own.

If sections of forest can be restored and left undisturbed, the tamarins may recover.

 Q: Who decides when an animal is endangered?

A: The IUCN (International Union for the Conservation of Nature and Natural Resources) co-ordinates research about surviving plant and animal families. The status of each species is assessed and the findings are published in Red Data Books. The buying, selling, hunting and poaching of wild animals is monitored by CITES (Convention on International Trade in Endangered Species of Wild Fauna and Flora).

Golden lion tamarins are tiny primates brought back from the brink. They have been bred in zoos, and many have now been returned to their natural home in Brazil's rainforests (above).

30

Glossary

Alien animal
An animal that is in a place other than its natural home, often introduced there by humans.

Ape
A higher primate with no tail, such as a gorilla.

Camouflage
The way in which an animal hides from predators by blending with its surroundings.

Captive breeding
The breeding of animals in zoos and parks to preserve endangered species.

Endangered
Describes an animal in danger of extinction, whose survival is threatened if the reasons for its decline continue.

Extinct
Describes a species that has not been seen in the wild for the past 50 years.

Habitat
The place where an animal lives, usually characterised by the plants that grow there.

Logging
Cutting down trees for timber.

Marsupial
A pouched mammal from Australia, such as a kangaroo.

Monkey
A primate with a large brain and a tail.

Monotreme
A mammal that lays eggs.

Oriental medicine
A form of medicine from the Far East that uses parts of plants and animals to help prevent or cure diseases.

Plantation
A stand of trees or other plants that are planted by people in order to harvest their wood, leaves or fruits.

Poaching
The illegal hunting and trapping of animals.

Population
A group of individuals of the same type.

Predator
An animal that hunts and eats other animals.

Primate
A mainly tree-living mammal with a well-developed brain, forward-facing eyes, mobile hands and quick reactions.

Rainforest
A wooded area where rainfall is extremely high. Tropical rainforests include those in the Amazon and Congo.

Range
The area in which an animal lives for most of its life, including places it visits often.

Species
Animals that resemble one another closely and are able to breed together.

Subspecies
Animals of the same species that have developed their own characteristics, often because they have been separated from others with which they could breed.

31

Index